Charting New Horizons
Women Innovators and Entrepreneurs

Melinda Frances Graham

Table of Contents

1. Introduction 2
2. Breaking Ground: Early Women Innovators and Entrepreneurs .. 3
    2.1. Before the Industrial Revolution: Pioneers in Obscurity 3
    2.2. The Shaping of Industry and Commerce: Women Innovators of the Industrial Revolution 4
    2.3. The Rise of Women Entrepreneurs: Emergence of a New Economic Force 4
    2.4. World War II: Unleashing the True Potential of Women 4
    2.5. Post-War Persistence: Sustained Momentum in the Face of Resurging Patriarchy 5
3. Overcoming Hurdles: Challenges Faced by Women in Innovation and Entrepreneurship 6
    3.1. The Glass Ceiling: A Translucent but Tangible Barrier 6
    3.2. Limited Access to Capital: A Persistent Stumbling Block 7
    3.3. Sociocultural Norms and Biases: Unseen but Impenetrable Barriers 7
    3.4. Contravening the Work-Life Balance Dilemma 8
4. The Innovation Imperative: Profiles of Women Innovators Making a Difference 10
    4.1. The Technological Trailblazers 10
    4.2. The Social Innovators 11
    4.3. The Business Innovators 11
    4.4. The Science and Health Innovators 12
5. Unlocking Potential: Deconstructing the Journey of Successful Women Entrepreneurs 13
    5.1. Sub Chapter Heading: The Starting Point: Seeds of an Entrepreneurial Mindset 13
    5.2. Sub Chapter Heading: Mapping the Path: Preparing the

    Terrain and Planting the Idea 14
    5.3. Sub Chapter Heading: The Growth Stage: Nurturing the
    Venture through Challenges 14
    5.4. Sub Chapter Heading: The Flowering: Seeing Fruits of
    Labor and Making an Impact 15
    5.5. Sub Chapter Heading: Paving the Way: Inspiring the Next
    Generation 16
6. Silicon Valley She-oes: Women Leaders in Tech Start-ups 17
    6.1. The Winds of Change: Rise of Women in Silicon Valley 17
    6.2. Pioneering Innovation and Driving Technology 18
    6.3. Trends, Opportunities, and Future Prospects 18
    6.4. The Path Forward: Building a More Inclusive Ecosystem 19
7. Advancing Inclusivity: Policies and Best Practices Promoting
Gender Equality 20
    7.1. Gender Inequality in Business: A Global Overview 20
    7.2. Pushing Legislation: Policy Effects on Gender Equality 21
    7.3. Best Practices: Notable Strategies Across Global Enterprises . 22
    7.4. The Way Forward: Policies and Practices Encouraging
    Future Growth 22
8. Wielders of Resilience: How Women Entrepreneurs Adapt and
Overcome 24
    8.1. The Resilience Paradigm 24
    8.2. Tireless Adaptability in the Face of Resistance 24
    8.3. Embracing Failure: A Step Toward Success 25
    8.4. Cultivating Resilience: Examples to Emulate 25
    8.5. Leveraging Support Systems to Foster Resilience 26
9. The Frontier of Social Entrepreneurship: Women Lead the Way . 28
    9.1. Pioneers at the Frontline: Meet the Women Leading Social
    Change 28
    9.2. Rendering the Invisible, Visible: The Women Harnessing

Unseen Potential 29
9.3. The Tool Box: Skills and Knowledge that Drive Women
Entrepreneurs 29
9.4. The Twist in the Tale: Unique Challenges Faced by Women
Social Entrepreneurs 30
9.5. Kindling Change: Reshaping the Landscape for Women
Social Entrepreneurs 30
9.6. Conclusion: A New Dawn Beckons 31
10. The Global Stage: International Perspectives on Women in
Innovation and Entrepreneurship 32
10.1. The Cultural Canvas: A Broad Spectrum of Global
Perspectives 32
10.2. The Global Players: Women Visionaries from around the
World 33
10.3. Tackling Taboos: From Societal Restrictions to Economic
Empowerment 33
10.4. Evolution of International Legislation: Seismic Shifts in
Policy and Governance 34
10.5. The Power of Collaboration: International Networks and
Support Structures 34
11. Futures Forged: Toward A New Era of Women's Innovation
and Entrepreneurship 36
11.1. A Constellation of Pioneering Spirits 36
11.2. The Lever of Educational Advancements 37
11.3. Entrepreneurship that Transcends Boundaries 37
11.4. Business Innovations in the Social Sphere 38
11.5. Policy Reforms - The Road to Gender Equality 38
11.6. Power of Resilience – Women Rising from the Ashes 38

I never dreamed about success, I worked for it.

— Estée Lauder

Chapter 1. Introduction

Unveiling the curtains on a compelling narrative, this special report, "Charting New Horizons: Women Innovators and Entrepreneurs" celebrates stories of female ingenuity, resiliency, and transformative thought in the world of business. Wrapped in the fabric of both struggle and triumph, these women have forged paths, shattered glass ceilings, and have become a beacon of inspiration for generations to come. Anticipate a harmonious blend of insightful profiles, robust data, thought-provoking analysis, and profound lessons that trace the remarkable journey of women leaders who have dared to tread beyond the ordinary. If you're seeking an illuminating read that ushers motivation, challenges convention, and champions the spirit of audacious innovation, this report is an essential addition to your collection.

Chapter 2. Breaking Ground: Early Women Innovators and Entrepreneurs

The onset of women's influence on the frontiers of innovation and entrepreneurship dates back hundreds, if not thousands, of years. Beginning in an era when they were typically assigned roles within the domestic sphere, the journey of early women innovators and entrepreneurs is soaked in transformative resilience, dogged determination and an undying spirit of rebellion against the status quo.

2.1. Before the Industrial Revolution: Pioneers in Obscurity

Before the dawn of the Industrial Revolution, women's innovative efforts and entrepreneurial ventures operated primarily under the radar to the wider society that largely ignored or suppressed their achievements. Yet, their impact was undeniably significant. Women engaged in myriad underappreciated roles, acting as herbalists, midwives, and brewers, contributing to the growth of society behind the scenes. One notable woman was Trotula of Salerno, an 11th-century Italian physician who penned seminal texts on women's health, gynecology, and cosmetics, defying societal norms while innovating within a strictly male-dominated field.

2.2. The Shaping of Industry and Commerce: Women Innovators of the Industrial Revolution

With the advent of the Industrial Revolution, a profound shift of societal dynamics sprouted, resulting in visible, pioneering efforts by women. Take Sarah Guppy, an English inventor awarded a patent in 1809 for a method of making safe piling for bridges, a technique used in constructing the globally celebrated Clifton Suspension Bridge. Or Margaret Knight, the American inventor known for her patent in 1871 of a machine that could produce flat-bottomed paper bags, an invention that fundamentally transformed the retail industry.

2.3. The Rise of Women Entrepreneurs: Emergence of a New Economic Force

Parallel to their impact on innovation, women were also paving the way in entrepreneurship. Madame C.J. Walker, an African American entrepreneur, philanthropist, and political and social activist, started her line of cosmetics and hair care products for black women in the late 19th to early 20th century, becoming one of the first female self-made millionaires in America. Her story illustrates the courage and tenacity of women who broke societal and racial barriers to achieve unprecedented success.

2.4. World War II: Unleashing the True Potential of Women

World War II acted as an inflection point for women in innovation and entrepreneurship. As men went off to war, women's skills were essential to maintaining the economy. They stepped into roles previously deemed only suitable for men, from manufacturing and engineering to science and programming. Women like Hedy Lamarr, an Austrian-born American actress who also co-invented a frequency-hopping spread spectrum that is a building block of today's wifi, GPS, and Bluetooth technologies, shone brightly during this era.

2.5. Post-War Persistence: Sustained Momentum in the Face of Resurging Patriarchy

After the war, despite the enormous achievements they made in the absence of men, women found themselves being pushed back into the traditional roles of the pre-war society. Yet, they continued their stride in innovation and entrepreneurship. The story of Grace Hopper, a brilliant mathematician and computer scientist who invented the first compiler and laid the groundwork for the development of COBOL, illustrates persistence in the face of prevalent societal odds.

This chapter has shed light on the remarkable founding history of women innovators and entrepreneurs. From their invisible work prior to the industrial revolution, their transformative roles during the industrial age, their groundbreaking ventures in entrepreneurship, their indispensable service in World War II, and their persistence amidst the post-war societal shift, women have been etching their places in the world of innovation and entrepreneurship from the deepest pages of history. Their legacies serve as profound inspiration and beckon us towards a future where such achievements are not the exception but rather the norm.

Chapter 3. Overcoming Hurdles: Challenges Faced by Women in Innovation and Entrepreneurship

The world of innovation and entrepreneurship is invigorating, filled with opportunities, and is the bedrock of economic progress. Yet, the journey towards such progress is fraught with obstacles, more so for women, whose path to success is often intertwined with a labyrinth of unique challenges. This chapter sets out to dissect the prevalent hurdles that are specific to women in the realms of innovation and entrepreneurship, shedding light upon the barriers, both overt and covert, that have impeded female progress in these pivotal sectors.

3.1. The Glass Ceiling: A Translucent but Tangible Barrier

Entering the entrepreneurial realm presents itself with countless intricacies and hardships. However, one of the most pervasive systemic issues dogging women entrepreneurs is the existence of the so-called 'glass ceiling'. It essentially represents an unassailable barrier preventing women from rising to top executive positions within their organizations, regardless of their qualifications or achievements. This invisible yet formidable obstacle intensifies as women strive to ascend the corporate ladder, their capacity for leadership frequently overlooked or outright dismissed due to entrenched societal biases.

The glass ceiling effect is not relinquished to the confines of the corporate world alone, but extends to the entrepreneurial world as well. An underrepresentation of women in leadership positions within start-ups, as well as in the technology and innovation sector, is conspicuously apparent. This has created an insidious feedback loop of a male-dominated industry reluctant to integrate and accommodate diverse perspectives, thereby reinforcing a culture that stifles female entrepreneurship.

3.2. Limited Access to Capital: A Persistent Stumbling Block

One of the most formidable challenges faced by women entrepreneurs is the issue of capital acquisition. There is a striking discrepancy in funding between businesses led by men and those helmed by women. Data reveals that women-led startups receive significantly less venture capital than those led by their male counterparts. This gender disparity is propagated by a distressing combination of ingrained biases and stereotypes within the investment industry, where decisions are sometimes driven by preconceived notions rather than the merit of business proposals.

Limited access to capital poses a stifling effect on the proliferation of women-led businesses. It hampers their ability to develop, expand, and compete effectively within the market. Moreover, this can dissuade potential women entrepreneurs from pursuing their innovative ideas, thereby cutting short their entrepreneurial journey even before it begins.

3.3. Sociocultural Norms and Biases: Unseen but Impenetrable Barriers

Deep-rooted societal stereotypes and cultural norms pose substantial barriers to women's progress in innovation and entrepreneurship. Traditional norms that dictate gender roles can undermine women's confidence and assertiveness requisite for leadership roles. Societal preconceptions often question the capability of women to effectively perform in high-risk environments, thereby undermining their authority and discouraging their participation in innovative and entrepreneurial undertakings.

Bias, whether conscious or unconscious, continues to plague entrepreneurial ecosystems worldwide, influencing perceptions about women's capabilities and resulting in their marginalization. These biases are not limited to external entities but are often internalized by women themselves, triggering self-doubt and hesitancy in embracing entrepreneurial ambitions. This systematically dampens the entrepreneurial spirit among women, leading to a startling dearth of female innovators and entrepreneurs.

3.4. Contravening the Work-Life Balance Dilemma

A conflict that has perennially surrounded female entrepreneurial discourse is the struggle to strike a balance between personal and professional responsibilities. The societal expectations that envision women as primary caregivers often put them at a disadvantage when it comes to committing to entrepreneurial pursuits. Maintaining this elusive balance becomes even more difficult as a business owner, considering the unpredictable and often demanding nature of entrepreneurial ventures.

The resultant stress from juggling multiple roles can undermine their mental health, and in some cases, lead to burnout, hampering productivity and dampening creativity. This incessantly revolving cycle not only deters women from initiating entrepreneurial journeys but also hinders those in the course to reach their full potential.

This chapter encapsulates the intricate web of persistent challenges faced by women in innovation and entrepreneurship, each emerging from a complex intersection of societal norms, systemic barriers, and personal hurdles. Recognition of these issues is the first step towards eradication. As we navigate through this perceptive exploration, a clarion call is made for collective action to dismantle these barriers, foster an inclusive environment supporting women's entrepreneurial journey, and pave the way towards an egalitarian landscape for innovation and entrepreneurship.

Chapter 4. The Innovation Imperative: Profiles of Women Innovators Making a Difference

As we delve into our deep-dive examination of the innovation imperative and women's leading role in shaping it, we witness an incredible tableau of transformation and impact. It is here that we profile the trailblazing women who through their perspicacity and tenacity, have resolutely made a significant difference in their fields.

4.1. The Technological Trailblazers

We begin our exploration with women who have carved their niche in the realm of technology, often a predominantly male domain. Highlighting the tale of brilliance is Dr. Mae Jemison, a physician, engineer, and NASA astronaut who overcame adversity to become the first African American woman to travel in space. Not confined to just space travel, she invested her intellect and innovative vision into health-related technology solutions that bridged medical science with engineering, impacting global health positively.

Next on our roster of luminaries is Shafi Goldwasser, a pioneer in the field of cryptography. Her groundbreaking work in probabilistic encryption has revolutionized online communications, making it robust and secure in an era of ever-increasing digital connectivity. Goldwasser's trailblazing work in zero-knowledge proof has been monumental in establishing secure digital identities and ensuring blockchain integrity, curating a new playing field for robust cybersecurity.

4.2. The Social Innovators

Defining innovation beyond the contours of technology, we shift focus to those courageous women who dared to challenge societal norms, thus scripting transformative narratives. Malala Yousafzai, a prominent advocate for equal education, has demonstrated what it means to be a compelling social innovator. Despite facing potentially life-ending violence, her courageous stand against oppression and advocacy for girls education has revolutionized attitudes towards women's entitlement to knowledge and upliftment.

Equally noteworthy is Greta Thunberg, who, at a very tender age, gave voice to the looming climate crisis. Her unwavering commitment to the cause of environment and climate change awareness has spurred global action, proving that innovation is not always about creating new technology, but can also be about understanding and solving the most pressing problems facing humanity.

4.3. The Business Innovators

Let's now turn our attention to the business arena, a field where women have consistently proven their mettle as innovators and leaders. Mary Barra, the CEO of General Motors, is a prime example. Being the first female CEO of a major global automaker, Barra's focus on environmental sustainability and electric vehicles has helped rejuvenate an aging industry and cement her reputation as a staunch innovator.

We also honour the ingenuity of Indra Nooyi, former CEO of PepsiCo. Her innovative leadership strategy incorporated long-term sustainable growth, addressing health concerns related to the company's products and committing to ambitious environmental sustainability targets. With her forward-thinking approach, Nooyi reinvented the landscape of the global food and beverage industry.

4.4. The Science and Health Innovators

Shifting the focus towards the invaluable contributions of women in science and healthcare, we present visionary innovators such as Jennifer Doudna and Emmanuelle Charpentier, renowned for developing CRISPR gene-editing technology. Their unprecedented work has revolutionized genetic research, with the potential to eradicate genetic diseases and ensure better health outcomes.

Highlighting the contemporary COVID-19 scenario, we celebrate the work of Dr. Kizzmekia Corbett, an instrumental figure in developing the Moderna vaccine. Dr. Corbett's platform in vaccine technology not only brought forth a solution to an emergent global crisis but also iterated the importance of revolutionary thinking in responding to public-health emergencies.

Moving deftly from the historical landscape towards the contemporary and future-scape, this chapter elucidates the extraordinary contributions and compelling individual narratives of these women. Often navigating through unchartered territories and confronting adversities, these women innovators have paved the way for a more inclusive, equitable and prosperous future. As each story unfolds, a paradigm of audacious innovation and transformative thinking reflects, enriching our understanding of the profound impact of women in shaping our world today. They underline the criticality of the innovation imperative in our society, underlining the fact that diversity and inclusivity within this space aren't just desirable, but absolutely essential.

Chapter 5. Unlocking Potential: Deconstructing the Journey of Successful Women Entrepreneurs

The journey of entrepreneurship is akin to a labyrinth; it is fraught with roadblocks, dead ends, and detours, yet it is also brimming with thrilling discoveries, sudden breakthroughs, and rewarding victories. To be a woman navigating this labyrinth adds another layer of complexity, which is not merely an underrepresentation tale but a well-crafted narrative of outwitting stereotypes, challenging society's expectations, and rising above adversity. Still, it is essential to identify that such journeys are far from homogeneous; distinct in their rhythm, modulated by experiences, and tuned by personal and socio-cultural nuances.

5.1. Sub Chapter Heading: The Starting Point: Seeds of an Entrepreneurial Mindset

Embarking on the entrepreneurial journey often begins with a seed: an idea, a passion, a curiosity that blossoms into a vision. Many successful women entrepreneurs have shared the recurring theme of seeing a gap in the market, spotting an unmet need, or simply wanting to make a change. Sometimes, it is a personal experience or a deeply rooted passion that triggers the entrepreneurial pursuit.

Take the example of Judith Faulkner; the founder of Epic Systems Corporation, a healthcare software company. Her journey began when she identified that the existing healthcare records system was inefficient and sought to create a digital alternative. Or consider Sara Blakely, the founder of Spanx, who was motivated by her personal travails to design undergarments that provided the needed comfort and support for women.

5.2. Sub Chapter Heading: Mapping the Path: Preparing the Terrain and Planting the Idea

Once the entrepreneurial seed is sown, it needs to be nurtured with careful planning, preparation, and ultimately, action. Preparation typically takes the form of extensive market research, identifying prospective customers, and understanding the competitive landscape which lays the groundwork for their business plan. This phase also entails identifying sources of funding, which for many women, presents their first significant hurdle due to gender-discrimination often faced in conventional funding avenues.

Crowdfunding platforms and microfinance institutions have emerged as alternative funding options. These carry the promise of democratizing access to capital and allowing more women to plant their entrepreneurial seeds. Platforms like Kiva and Kickstarter have had stories of women leveraging them to secure necessary funding.

5.3. Sub Chapter Heading: The Growth Stage: Nurturing the Venture through Challenges

This stage of the journey is defined by many vital activities: building a team, developing a product or service, reaching out to customers, maintaining quality, scaling the operations, and most importantly, sustaining the business through challenges. Often, the entrepreneur is not just the CEO but dons many hats - marketer, HR, customer care rep, and even bookkeeper.

Unfortunately, women often face bias and discrimination that can hinder growth. A study by The Boston Consulting Group and MassChallenge, a global network of accelerators, found that businesses founded by women deliver higher revenue—more than twice as much per dollar invested—than those founded by men. However, they also discovered that women-founded startups received less funding. There's a profound need to address these biases that become a recurrent theme in women's entrepreneurial journeys to foster a truly inclusive environment.

5.4. Sub Chapter Heading: The Flowering: Seeing Fruits of Labor and Making an Impact

One of the most rewarding stages is when the entrepreneur starts to see the fruits of her labor. This not only reaffirms the entrepreneur's belief in her pursuit but also serves to inspire others, especially those women and girls who might see themselves in her journey.

A seminal study revealed that women entrepreneurs tend to create businesses that are purpose-driven, aiming to produce a positive impact on people's lives or to incite significant changes in their respective industries. Such businesses often focus on social, economical, and environmental sustainability, reflecting not only individual success but also creating a powerful, positive ripple effect in the community.

5.5. Sub Chapter Heading: Paving the Way: Inspiring the Next Generation

The ultimate triumph is a world where women's ventures are not an exception but a norm. Every successful woman entrepreneur automatically becomes a role model, inspiring other women to realize their entrepreneurial dreams. They become the pace-setters, the norm-challengers, the bias-shatterers, and the horizon-extenders. They inspire the next generation of women entrepreneurs by showing them the immense possibilities that await once they dare to dream and act.

In the end, it's not just about financial gain or business growth; it's about creating options and breaking down barriers. It's about showing the world the power of a woman with a dream and the determination to make it a reality. Each woman's journey is a torch in the darkness, igniting paths and inspiring change, one venture at a time. And, but of course, no two torches burn the same - the spirit might be similar, but the flame dances to its own mischievous tune, painting a fascinating display of resilience, innovation, and sheer audacity.

Chapter 6. Silicon Valley She-oes: Women Leaders in Tech Start-ups

The universe of technology and start-ups, which, for quite too long, had been governed predominantly by male intellects, is witnessing a drastic shift as more women leaders emerge to claim the tokens of leadership and authority. These are the charismatic women technologists who deafen the world's cynicism with their relentless pursuit of innovation and sustainability, propelling their tech start-ups to incredible heights.

6.1. The Winds of Change: Rise of Women in Silicon Valley

The emergence of women leaders in Silicon Valley marks the advent of an era of unprecedented change, wherein the gender narrative is being redrawn, driven by sheer resilience, willpower, and intellect. Take for instance, Marissa Mayer, known for her seminal stint at Yahoo Inc. She took the reins amidst tumultuous times and brought significant changes in culture and policy that reflected her vision for an inclusive work environment. Then there is Susan Wojcicki, the CEO of YouTube, who has been instrumental in driving the platform's phenomenal global reach.

Encountering and overcoming the challenges associated with a traditionally male-dominated field, these women continue to break barriers, inspiring many others in their stride. They constitute a powerful yet frequently overlooked force, driving evolution in the silicon heartland of the world.

6.2. Pioneering Innovation and Driving Technology

The tech start-ups led by women in Silicon Valley are not just products of their creative pursuits, but immersive projects that challenge the routines, dare the orthodoxies, and inspire transformation - a blend of innovative thought and pragmatic action.

Hosting success narratives are tech ventures such as Canva, led by Melanie Perkins, which has revolutionized the domain of visual communication, democratizing the process of design and enabling people with no technical skills to create stunning visuals.

Similarly, Anne Wojcicki's 23andMe has materialized the dream of making personalized healthcare a reality for the common man. Even as the tech giant faces challenges, with regulatory barriers and issues of accuracy and privacy, under Anne's astute leadership, the promise to democratize genetic information remains strong.

6.3. Trends, Opportunities, and Future Prospects

While the rise of women in Silicon Valley marks a significant shift, there is still much work to be done. As per a 2020 report by Silicon Valley Bank, women hold only 42% of executive positions in start-ups and only 40% of start-ups have a woman on their board of directors.

Yet, the silver lining is bright. Meg Whitman, former CEO of Hewlett Packard Enterprise, perceives that embracing women's thought leadership can be a catalyst for creativity and diversity that fosters innovation and drives superior performance.

The challenges are indeed enormous, but as the success narratives mentioned before suggest, they are not insurmountable. The future prospects for women in tech start-ups look promising, enhanced by diversity initiatives, increasing gender parity in STEM education, and the growing recognition of the immense value that women bring to the table.

6.4. The Path Forward: Building a More Inclusive Ecosystem

Any discourse on Silicon Valley's women leaders in tech start-ups would be incomplete without discussing the imperative need to establish a more inclusive ecosystem that fosters and encourages women's participation. Sheryl Sandberg's "Lean In" philosophy is an exemplary reference for advocating gender equality at workplace.

Such a solution should include measures to ensure equal pay, opportunities for growth, and recognition of work done by women. It is incumbent upon present leaders, both men and women, to spearhead such initiatives and set a precedent for future generations.

In conclusion, the narrative of women leaders in Silicon Valley start-ups is not just a narrative of success, but it is a testimony of courage, resilience, and transformative thought. Each victory gives rise to hope - a hope that the bastion of Silicon Valley, once notorious for the dearth of women in leadership positions, will soon bear witness to an environment of greater inclusivity and radical innovation propelled by the robust contribution of women. The future, indeed, seems poised for a new dawn where the 'She-oes' of Silicon Valley ascend to a well-deserved central stage.

Chapter 7. Advancing Inclusivity: Policies and Best Practices Promoting Gender Equality

The pivotal narrative revealed in this manual, "Charting New Horizons: Women Innovators and Entrepreneurs," is punctuated by numerous accounts that delve into the core of gender inclusion and diversity in economic and entrepreneurial realms. Cornerstone to this exploration is the notion of 'Advancing Inclusivity,' which contemplates the various policies, methodologies, and notable practices being applied across the globe to bridge the gender gap in business effectively. This pivotal chapter resolutely upholds and emphasizes the admirable pursuit and realization of gender equality.

7.1. Gender Inequality in Business: A Global Overview

The first exercise in pursuing inclusivity and equality within the business world involves grappling with the existing realities surrounding gender inequality. It is critical to dissect the societal structures and norms that hinder the progression of women within the innovative and entrepreneurial circles. These challenges could range from patriarchal biases, limited access to capital and resources, and lack of representation to subtle aspects such as stereotype threat and impostor syndrome.

Detailed evaluation of global surveys, statistics, and reports, such as those from the World Bank, the United Nations, and other international bodies, reveal a glaring disparity in the representation and success rates between male and female innovators and entrepreneurs. The vastness of this divide becomes even more conspicuous when examining the stories of women facing compounded biases due to intersecting social identities like race, age, and economic status.

Despite the gaining momentum for parity and social justice movements worldwide, an irrefutable reality remains: women face unique, severe obstacles in attaining their professional pursuits. These rampant inequities necessitate comprehensive strategies and policies that would serve to ameliorate these conditions and cultivate a more inclusive, balanced environment.

7.2. Pushing Legislation: Policy Effects on Gender Equality

Government legislation plays a crucial role in advancing gender equality on a broad scale. From policies promoting equal wage practices to laws regulating parental leave, affirmative action, and stipulations around venture capital investment; government intervention can significantly tilt the scales toward a more balanced, equitable playing field.

Inclusivity-promoting policies across the globe differ vastly, reflecting the socio-cultural, legal, and political contexts of different nations. For instance, Scandinavian countries are globally celebrated for their progressive policies, particularly those offering extensive parental leave and child care provisions. In comparison, the so-called 'Anglo-Saxon model,' adopted by countries like UK, USA, and Australia, has historically yielded more variations and has been slower in endorsing comprehensive gender-equal benefits.

Policy successes and pitfalls from around the world serve as instructive case studies, both for existing companies striving for gender balance and advancements, and for emerging start-ups seeking to build a foundation of inclusivity from the onset.

7.3. Best Practices: Notable Strategies Across Global Enterprises

Ultimately, the push for gender equality extends beyond the realm of policy and into the heart of the organizational structure. In pursuit of fostering an inclusive environment, many businesses globally have adopted commendable best practices that hold valuable insights for others.

From robust mentorship programs, professional development resources, and women leadership networks to balanced recruitment strategies, these businesses have demonstrated a clear and often fruitful commitment to gender inclusion. Evaluation of these strategies—a list that includes initiatives from global giants like IBM, Google, and Unilever—provides tangible lessons and strategies for other organizations on their journey towards inclusivity.

In-depth analyses of these policies, practices, and their outcomes drive home the reality that advancing inclusivity is not only an ethical imperative but also provides a competitive edge. Evidence abounds in favor of a diverse workforce driving innovation, broadening consumer understanding, and enhancing company culture.

7.4. The Way Forward: Policies and Practices Encouraging Future Growth

The journey toward greater gender equality in the world of business is far from over. However, the lessons garnered from examining various policies and practices serve as pivotal building blocks in constructing an inclusive future.

Promising trends on the horizon include the incorporation of gamification in bias training, rise in the number of women-led venture capital firms, and societal shifts that are propelling a more egalitarian view of parental roles. These trends, along with further exploration of gender identity and intersectionality in business, offer fresh perspectives and innovative routes for future growth.

In conclustion, establishing a comprehensive, inclusive system that facilitates growth for all, regardless of gender, is a collective responsibility. For progress to persist, understanding the global landscape, learning from realized policies, and adapting successful practices will be integral to paving the way towards an equitable business world—an enlightened path that steers clear from discriminatory divides to foster unity, innovation, and prosperity.

Chapter 8. Wielders of Resilience: How Women Entrepreneurs Adapt and Overcome

In the realm of entrepreneurship, one quality outshines many others – resilience. In this chapter, we delve deep into the iron will, persistence, and tenacity of women entrepreneurs who have skillfully adapted and overcome numerous challenges to etch their mark in diverse industries.

8.1. The Resilience Paradigm

Resilience, as universally understood in the context of human behavior, refers to the wherewithal of a person to recover from difficulties, stresses, or tragedies, and carry forward with renewed strength or even a transformed outlook. In the world of business, this human quality takes on an expanded dimension. For women pioneering their path in entrepreneurship - a terrain intimately acquainted with obstacles and setbacks - resilience is both a tactical weapon and strategic masterstroke.

8.2. Tireless Adaptability in the Face of Resistance

In the journey of a woman entrepreneur, resistance often appears in many guises. It might manifest as discrimination based on gender, lack of funding, limited access to networking opportunities, work-life balance struggles, or simply the inherent riskiness and unpredictability of running a new business. Women, however, have demonstrated an uncanny aptitude to adapt to these resistances.

Their adaptation strategies have been as varied and unique as they are. Some have adopted the 'bootstrap' method, shoring up personal savings and local resources to fund their startups. Others have leveraged social media and digital platforms to reach a global audience and circumvent traditional marketing barriers. Importantly, countless have custom-created their balancing acts, integrating their personal lives and their entrepreneurial pursuits to form a synergy rather than a tug-of-war. The examples are endless and richly diverse, underlining the dexterity with which women entrepreneurs adapt and shape-shift to face the resistance they encounter.

8.3. Embracing Failure: A Step Toward Success

"'Failure is not the opposite of success, it's part of success'- Arianna Huffington"

In the entrepreneurial journey, failure is often a guide, not a foe. However, surmounting the crushing blow of a failed venture, personal criticism, or public dissatisfaction calls for extraordinary resilience. Women entrepreneurs are demonstrating how to transform these apparent defeats into stepping stones. They quickly learn from the missteps, readjust their plans, and yield better results in the future. Embracing failure is no small feat, but in many ways, it is the cornerstone of resilience in entrepreneurship.

8.4. Cultivating Resilience: Examples to Emulate

Across the world, there are innumerable examples of women entrepreneurs whose resilience stands as an inspiration. Consider the story of Ursula Burns, who rose from a New York City housing project to become the CEO of Xerox. Despite the immense hurdles she faced, she continuously adapted, persevered, and overcame her obstacles, displaying formidable resilience.

Or Jane Wurwand, the founder of Dermalogica, who started with just a suitcase of skincare products. Despite countless challenges, she built a billion-dollar business. Her relentless pursuit of her vision, courage in the face of adversities, and her ability to recover from setbacks are testament to her resilience.

The essential message from these stories is that cultivating resilience is neither an overnight act nor a response to a single devastating event. It's an ongoing process – a blend of learned skills, supportive surroundings, keen foresight, and a resolute belief in oneself.

8.5. Leveraging Support Systems to Foster Resilience

Apart from personal strength and conviction, external support systems also play a critical role in building resilience among women entrepreneurs. These include mentorship, networking platforms, women-oriented business programs, and inclusive policies. Such systems aid women in bouncing back from setbacks, offering both emotional encouragement and pragmatic advice. They also foster a community spirit, which can be a powerful bolstering factor against the isolation often experienced in entrepreneurial pursuits.

In conclusion, the stories of resilience among women entrepreneurs are many, and each brings unique insights and profound lessons. Their indomitable spirit of resilience shines as a beacon for others to follow. It is these women who bend and sway with the winds of adversity, yet never break, that will shape the landscape of entrepreneurship in the coming decades. Their journey, filled with adaptability and overcoming odds, underscores the essence of this chapter – that resilience can be the fuel that drives the engine of entrepreneurship for women.

Chapter 9. The Frontier of Social Entrepreneurship: Women Lead the Way

Diving into the rich tapestry of social entrepreneurship, we find a vibrant ensemble of women leading the charge, transforming societal norms and changing the face of business with their profound dedication to social impact. It is here that our exploration begins, on the frontier of social entrepreneurship where women are carving out essential and innovative solutions to tackle some of our world's most pressing problems.

9.1. Pioneers at the Frontline: Meet the Women Leading Social Change

From the bustling streets of Mumbai to the rustic farmlands of Africa, women are at the helm of entities that champion social change. Kiran Mazumdar-Shaw, the intrepid leader of India's multibillion-dollar biopharmaceutical firm Biocon, constantly pushes for healthcare accessibility in resource-strained communities. Striding ahead in the African continent, Bethlehem Tilahun Alemu, the founder of SoleRebels, presented the global market with eco-friendly shoes and clothing, creating employment opportunities and boosting economic stability back home in Ethiopia.

Such exemplars not only exemplify business acumen but also espouse a deeper commitment to societal enrichment. Their enterprises are masterclasses in the amalgamation of profit-making and social upliftment, signifying that financial success does not negate the responsibility towards societal growth.

9.2. Rendering the Invisible, Visible: The Women Harnessing Unseen Potential

Social entrepreneurship uniquely involves harnessing unseen or unmet needs, and innumerable women have filled these gaps through innovative approaches. Chetna Sinha's Mann Deshi Bank in India, tailored for rural women, serves an untapped market while empowering its clients towards financial independence. Likewise, Iba Masood's AI startup, TARA, ensures access to freelance tech talent in parts of the world usually overlooked by traditional employment channels.

These novel problem-solving approaches defy the norm and require a sense of audacity that these women leaders have demonstrated multifold. The breakdown of traditional barriers in favor of new pathways underlines their ventures, proving the adaptability, and innovative capabilities of women in the realm of social entrepreneurship.

9.3. The Tool Box: Skills and Knowledge that Drive Women Entrepreneurs

While these women entrepreneurs are celebrated for their innovative solutions, it's instrumental to recognize the invaluable skills that serve as their bedrock. These include strategic vision, resilience, tenacity, and empathetic leadership. Moreover, a keen understanding of the community they serve, often borne from personal experience, amplifies their effectiveness.

Strategic vision and resilience, particularly, help these change makers weather the inevitable storms that accompany entrepreneurial undertakings. Their brave, tenacious outlook facilitates negotiations, funding procurement, and even cultural resistance. Empathetic leadership, on the other hand, builds trust, fosters team dynamics, and ensures stakeholders' interests align with the enterprise's social objective.

9.4. The Twist in the Tale: Unique Challenges Faced by Women Social Entrepreneurs

Despite the invaluable contributions of women entrepreneurs, they face an uphill battle, marred by entrenched sexism and lack of access to funding. The cultural trope of women being 'caregivers' rather than 'breadwinners' often undermines their professional credibility and limits their access to financial resources.

Even within the realm of social entrepreneurship, which fundamentally challenges the status quo, women constantly wrestle with gender biases. Often, their ventures are unfairly labeled as 'less ambitious,' viewing their social objectives as inconsistencies with profit-making rather than as coexisting objectives.

9.5. Kindling Change: Reshaping the Landscape for Women Social Entrepreneurs

Progress, however, is discernible. Business incubators, mentors, and funding platforms for women are sprouting, and laws are being recast to be more inclusive. Israel's WeAct, an entrepreneurial incubator for women, has been instrumental in fostering women-led social businesses. Investment initiative Golden Seeds devoted to investing in women-led businesses, and SheEO's global community model represent a growing trend in privileging women's entrepreneurial journeys.

Simultaneously, policy-level transformations are gradually leveling the playing field. With affirmative action movements such as the United Nations' Women's Empowerment Principles, the world is beginning to witness a paradigm shift towards an inclusive entrepreneurial ecosystem.

9.6. Conclusion: A New Dawn Beckons

As the chapter draws to a close, one fact remains indomitably clear: women, across geographies and contexts, are playing an instrumental role in the realm of social entrepreneurship. Their stories are a testimony to the power of creativity, relentlessness, and above all, conviction, in making a social impact. Their resolve to constructively challenge societal norms and innovate for good faces headwinds, but the dappled landscape of women's social entrepreneurship has never been more exciting or promising.

As we wrap up this extensive exploration, let us celebrate these women who stand at the threshold of revolutionizing our world – these harbingers of change who, imbued with courage and a burning desire to serve society, stand tall, their eyes firmly on the horizon, ready to lead the way.

Chapter 10. The Global Stage: International Perspectives on Women in Innovation and Entrepreneurship

As we lift the veil from a realm that transcends national boundaries, language barriers, and cultural hindrances, we get our first glimpse of how pioneering women across the globe have taken the stage in innovation and entrepreneurship. Ranging from sprawling metropolitan landscapes to remote rural enclaves, these stories are as varied as they are powerful, capturing the diverse range of experiences and perspectives of women who dared to challenge norms, shatter expectations, and deftly maneuver through the complexities and nuances of the global business environment.

10.1. The Cultural Canvas: A Broad Spectrum of Global Perspectives

Understanding international outlooks on women in innovation and entrepreneurship cannot be achieved without first acknowledging the intricacies of culture and societal norms that shape the landscape of opportunity and challenge. In Japan's highly reserved and hierarchical society, for instance, the pathway towards business leadership for women is often paved with comparative roadblocks. Whereas in entrepreneurial hotspots like Silicon Valley, women encounter different challenges, such as deeply-entrenched biases within the largely male-dominated tech sector. Thus, the cultural canvas upon which the narrative of women's contribution unfolds, exhibits a broad spectrum of varying perspectives, experiences, and environments that uniquely influence their entrepreneurial journey.

10.2. The Global Players: Women Visionaries from around the World

Within this diverse cornucopia of circumstances and cultures, emerge women who have written their own rules, innovated in their distinctive ways, and forged their unique paths to success. The indelible imprint of these visionaries can be discerned on the international business landscape. Consider the powerful influence of women like Jung Eun-ju, co-founder of South Korea's most popular navigation app, Naver. Or the transformative vision of Kiran Mazumdar-Shaw, the self-made biotech queen from India. Their careers serve as compelling narratives of resilience and creativity, illustrating the significant role of women in reshaping economies and societies across the globe.

10.3. Tackling Taboos: From Societal Restrictions to Economic Empowerment

While women innovators and entrepreneurs globally face an array of challenges, many of these trials are heavily embedded in societal and cultural constraints. In regions where traditional roles and expectations for women continue to hold firm their grip, overcoming these roadblocks becomes an imperative part of the journey towards success. By debunking myths and tearing down societal structures that restrict the economic empowerment of women, these change-makers have not only paved the way for improved gender equality in business but have also contributed significantly to economic growth and development.

10.4. Evolution of International Legislation: Seismic Shifts in Policy and Governance

Central to the narrative of women's global entrepreneurship are the transformative shifts in international legislation that accord women greater socioeconomic opportunities. Countries like New Zealand, Canada, and many European nations have demonstrated a commitment to establishing policies and legislation conducive to women's economic empowerment, thereby creating environments that nurture and foster female entrepreneurship and innovation.

10.5. The Power of Collaboration: International Networks and Support Structures

The establishment of international networks and support structures has provided criticial propulsion to women's global entrepreneurship journey. Institutions such as the Global Women Innovators and Inventors Network (GWIIN) have offered valuable mentorship, resources, and advocacy for women inventors, innovators, and entrepreneurs worldwide. These networks not only foster collaboration and exchange of ideas, but they also encourage more women to step into roles of business leadership, spurring a ripple effect of inspiration and empowerment across continents.

Drawing the curtains to a close on this journey around the world, the spirit of women's innovation and entrepreneurship is not merely confined within national borders or influenced solely by cultural contexts. Instead, it thrives in the synergistic interplay of multifarious global perspectives, from societal nuances and government policies to support structures and international collaboration. It is the collage of these diverse experiences, stories, and lessons that inspires and propels forward the narrative of women innovators and entrepreneurs on the global stage, forever pushing the horizons of possibility. The journey is arduous, the challenges significant, but the spirit of these women remains undaunted, their resilience unmatched, and their contribution pivotal to ushering us into a new era of innovation and entrepreneurship.

Chapter 11. Futures Forged: Toward A New Era of Women's Innovation and Entrepreneurship

Throughout history, women have been the catalyst of remarkable changes in various fields. It's the nexus of ingenuity, resilience, and transformative thought that has led to extraordinary feats achieved by women innovators and entrepreneurs. With this rich tapestry of their stories, there is a promising future that's being forged for them - a new era of innovative brilliance and entrepreneurial spirit rising from the cadence of past accomplishments.

11.1. A Constellation of Pioneering Spirits

As we embark on an exploration of the future, it is vital to recognize the collective impact of pioneering women who have charted the course of the past and the present. The diverse spectrum of inventiveness has been amplified as more women found their voices and made significant contributions in science, technology, mathematics, business, literature, and creative spheres. The progress attained is not merely an aggregation of individual success; it's a constellation, a testament of the relentless pioneering spirit of women across the world.

11.2. The Lever of Educational Advancements

Education has always been a powerful lever in empowering women, stimulating their innovative potential, and enhancing their business acumen. The future promises exponential expansion in the educational opportunities for women, with targeted training programs, scholarships, and initiatives to promote the inclusion of women in traditionally male-dominated fields like STEM. It has become bulletin-worthy news to learn that initiatives such as #ChooseScience campaign by UNESCO or the Technovation Challenge are being launched to encourage girls to pursue careers in science. The future appears to be poised with an era where educational opportunities will act as a catalyst for women's innovation and entrepreneurship.

11.3. Entrepreneurship that Transcends Boundaries

Women entrepreneurs are not just reshaping the business landscape, they are creating a global entrepreneurial ecosystem that transcends local, regional, and national boundaries. Indeed, we are forging a future where entrepreneurship knows no gender, ethnicity, or geographical constraints. Digital platforms, remote working possibilities, and online business models offer a myriad of opportunities for women to establish and grow their ventures. Global initiatives like the UN's SheTrades, which seeks to connect women entrepreneurs around the world, exemplify the limitless prospects of this new era.

11.4. Business Innovations in the Social Sphere

At the heart of this new era is not just economic gain but a profound urge to create social impact. Increasingly, women are leveraging their entrepreneurial ambitions to address social issues such as poverty, health care, education, and environmental sustainability. Social entrepreneurship represents a nexus where compassion meets innovation, and women are taking the vanguard position in shaping this space, with their businesses serving as engines of social change.

11.5. Policy Reforms - The Road to Gender Equality

The journey towards a new era of women's innovation and entrepreneurship also requires infrastructural support in the form of policy reforms. Governments, corporations, educational institutions, and NGOs engage in the collaborative and continuous effort to close the gender gap and create an environment where women's talents and competencies are recognized and rewarded equally. This positive trend is indicative of a future where policies are not just about promoting gender equality, but also about celebrating and nurturing the rich diversity of women innovators and entrepreneurs.

11.6. Power of Resilience – Women Rising from the Ashes

A transformative aspect that orchestrates the future of women's innovation and entrepreneurship is the influences drawn from their character and resilience. Through the annals of time, women have proven time and again their capacity to thrive amidst adversities, turning challenges into opportunities. These compelling narratives carry the testament that the power of resilience lies not in never failing, but in rising every time we fail. This undying spirit becomes a part of the genome of the future, where women continue to adapt, overcome, and flourish.

The future of women's innovation and entrepreneurship looks vibrant as we usher into an era painted with the hues of their relentless spirit. It's a journey that sees our global civilization evolve - breaking barriers, confronting stereotypes, and advancing towards inclusivity. It's not just an era of 'Women in Business.' It serves as a revolution that echoes the irresistible rhythm of women's capacity for creativity, courage, entrepreneurship, and resilience. Their narrative is not just a story of overcoming challenges but also an indomitable blueprint for the generations to come - the genesis of an era that champions the audacity of womanhood.

www.ingramcontent.com/pod-product-compliance
Lightning Source LLC
Chambersburg PA
CBHW070952220526
45471CB00007B/2999